JOURNEY THROUGH OUR SOLAR SYSTEM

EXPLORING PLUTO AND OTHER DWARF PLANETS

Published in 2018 by
KidHaven Publishing, an Imprint of Greenhaven Publishing, LLC
353 3rd Avenue
Suite 255
New York, NY 10010

Designer: Deanna Paternostro
Editor: Vanessa Oswald

Photo credits: Cover, p. 21 (background), back cover Vadim Sadovski/Shutterstock.com; pp. 4–5 Macrovector/Shutterstock.com; p. 7 NikNaks/Wikimedia Commons; p. 9 Elegant Solution/Shutterstock.com; p. 11 PlanetUser/Wikimedia Commons; p. 13 Kwamikagami/Wikimedia Commons; p. 15 Elenarts/Shutterstock.com; pp. 17, 21 (top) Drbogdan/Wikimedia Commons; p. 19 Reepy1/Wikimedia Commons; p. 21 (bottom) LROC/NASA/Wikimedia Commons.

Cataloging-in-Publication Data

Names: Lawrence, Riley.
Title: Exploring Pluto and other dwarf planets / Riley Lawrence.
Description: New York : KidHaven Publishing, 2018. | Series: Journey through our solar system | Includes index.
Identifiers: ISBN 9781534522909 (pbk.) | 9781534522800 (library bound) | ISBN 9781534522527 (6 pack) | ISBN 9781534522763 (ebook)
Subjects: LCSH: Dwarf planets–Juvenile literature. | Pluto (Dwarf planet)–Juvenile literature.
Classification: LCC QB701.L39 2018 | DDC 523.48'2–dc23
Printed in the United States of America

CPSIA compliance information: Batch #BS17KL: For further information contact Greenhaven Publishing LLC, New York, New York at 1-844-317-7404.

Please visit our website, www.greenhavenpublishing.com. For a free color catalog of all our high-quality books, call toll free 1-844-317-7404 or fax 1-844-317-7405.

CONTENTS

THE DWARF PLANET

Pluto was once seen as the smallest and most distant planet in the **solar system**.

Shown here are all the planets in the solar system and Pluto.

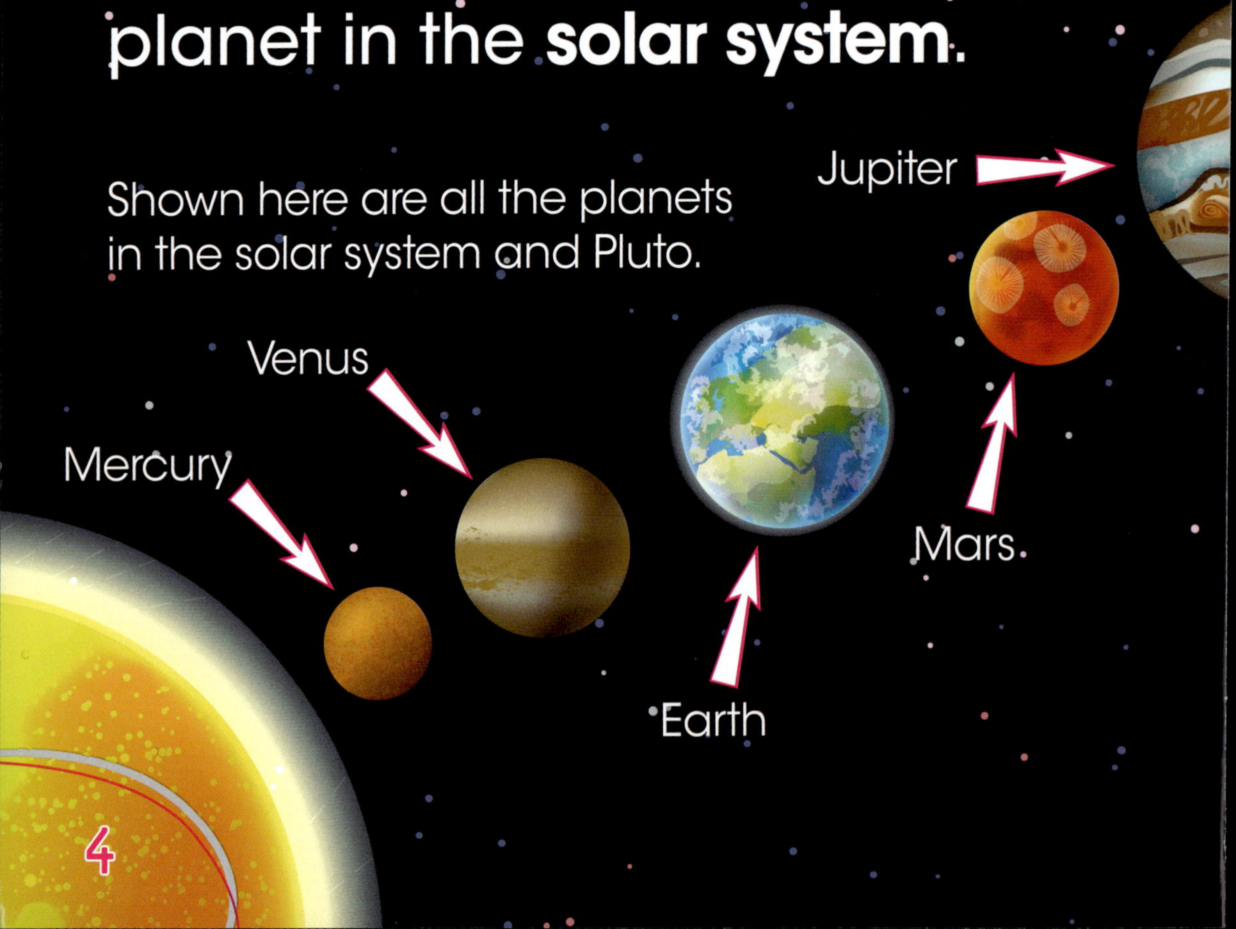

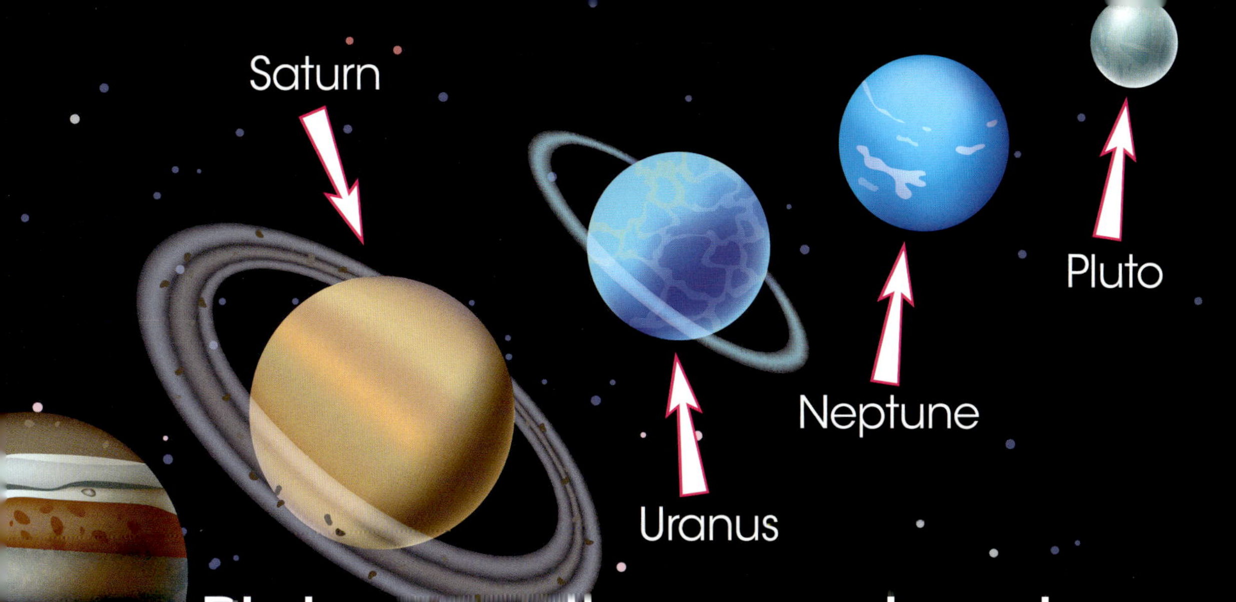

Pluto was discovered and named a planet in 1930. It was then given the title of a dwarf planet 76 years later. A dwarf planet is a space body that's too small to be called a planet.

The name "dwarf planets" was chosen because of the small size of these space bodies. Some of the first dwarf planets found were Eris, Ceres, Makemake, and Haumea. They're found in the **Kuiper Belt**, except for Ceres, which is in the **asteroid belt**.

Pluto is one of the largest dwarf planets.

FAR ORBIT

Pluto takes about 248 Earth years to **orbit** the sun. All the planets in the solar system orbit the sun. The only reason Pluto isn't called a planet is because of its smaller size. It's smaller than Earth's moon.

Pluto’s orbit, or path, around the sun is shown here.

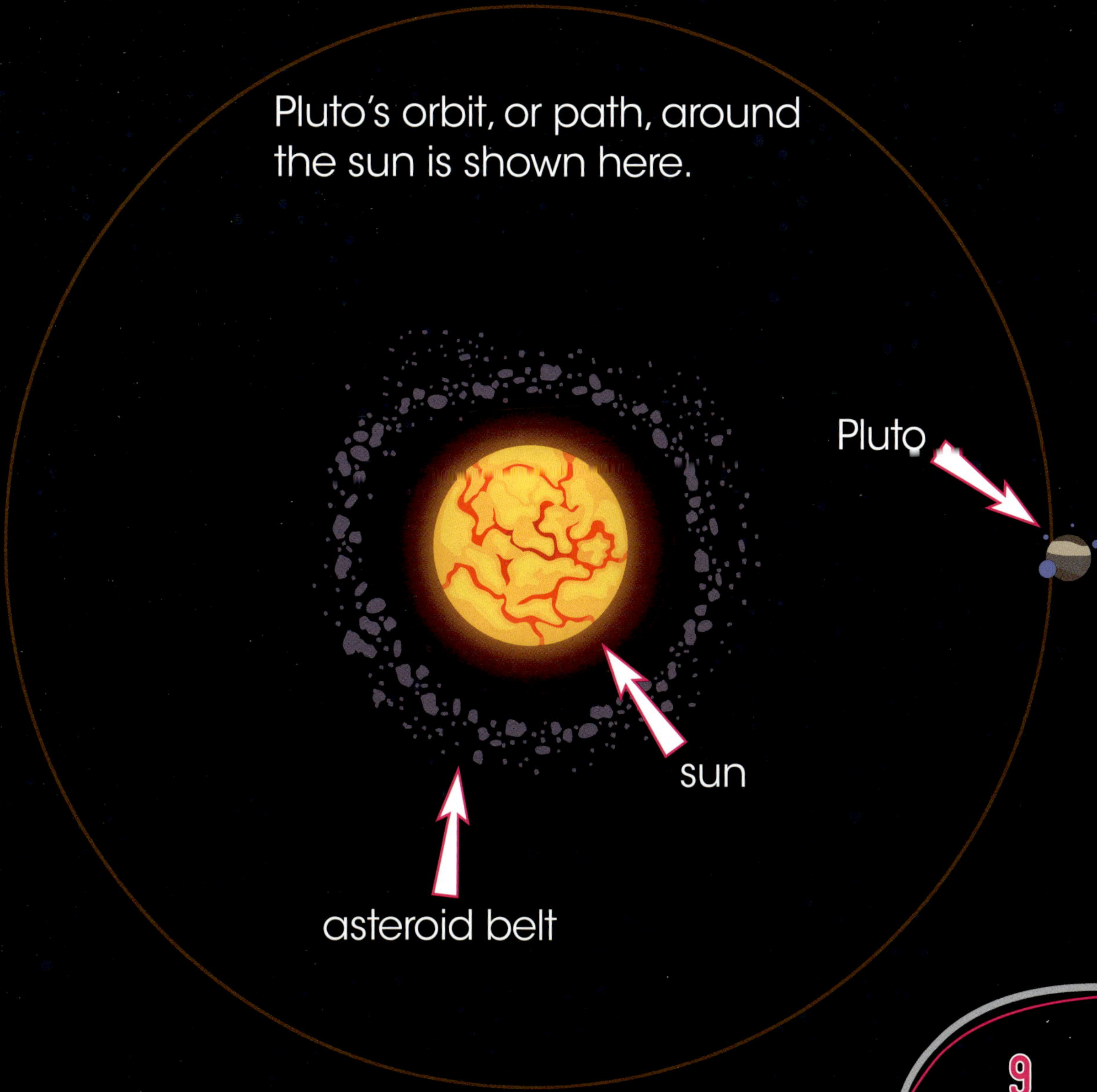

PLUTO'S LAYERS

Pluto has a **layer** of gases called an atmosphere that surrounds it. The dwarf planet's atmosphere is made up of the gases nitrogen, carbon monoxide, and methane. A thick layer of ice covers the ground, and under the ice is a rocky center.

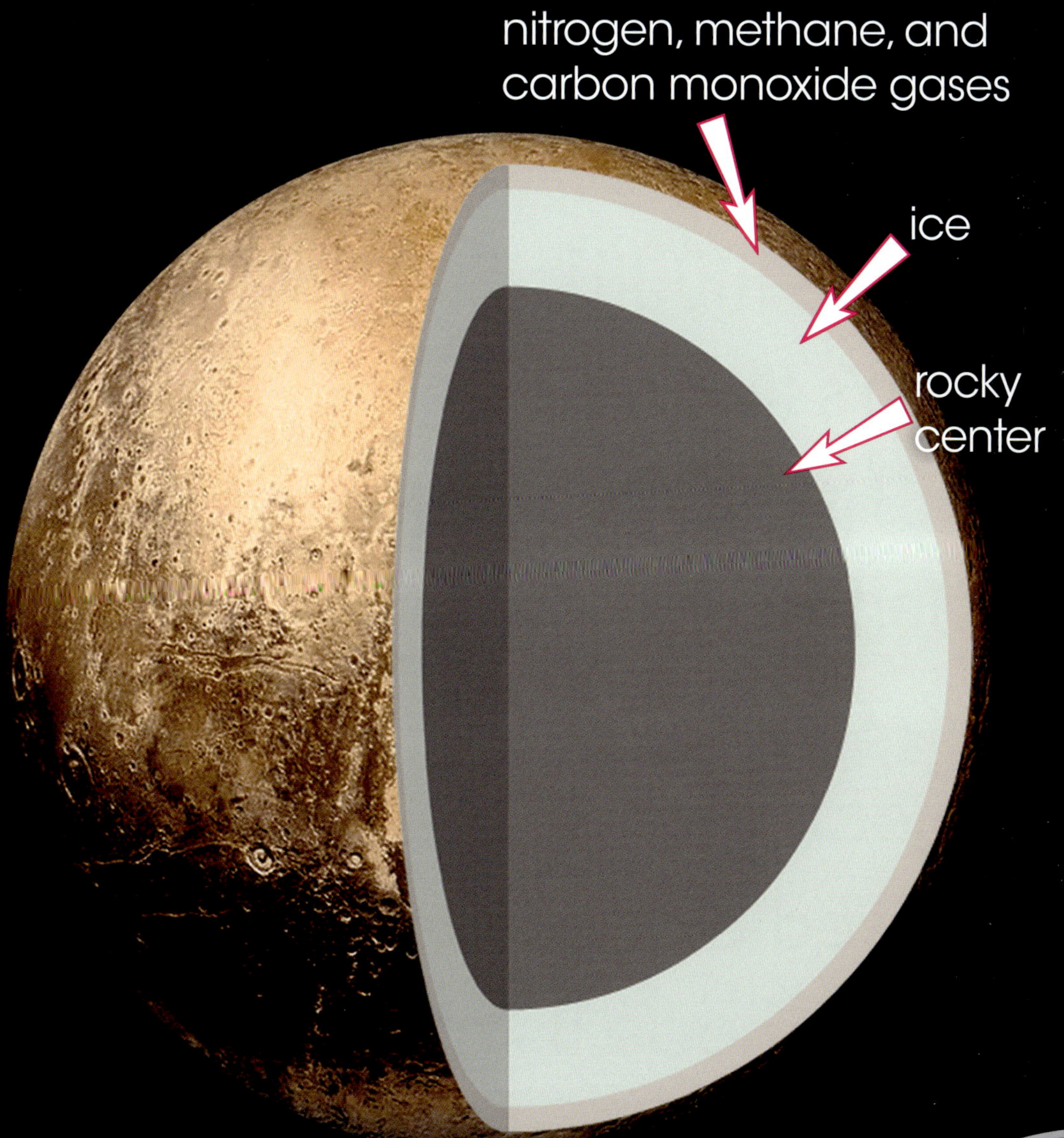

Shown here are
the layers of Pluto.

PLUTO'S MOONS

Pluto's five moons are Charon, Nix, Hydra, Kerberos, and Styx. Scientists think Pluto smashed into another planet-sized object a long time ago. This caused pieces to break off, which made its moons.

The ground of all five of Pluto's moons seems to be made of water and ice.

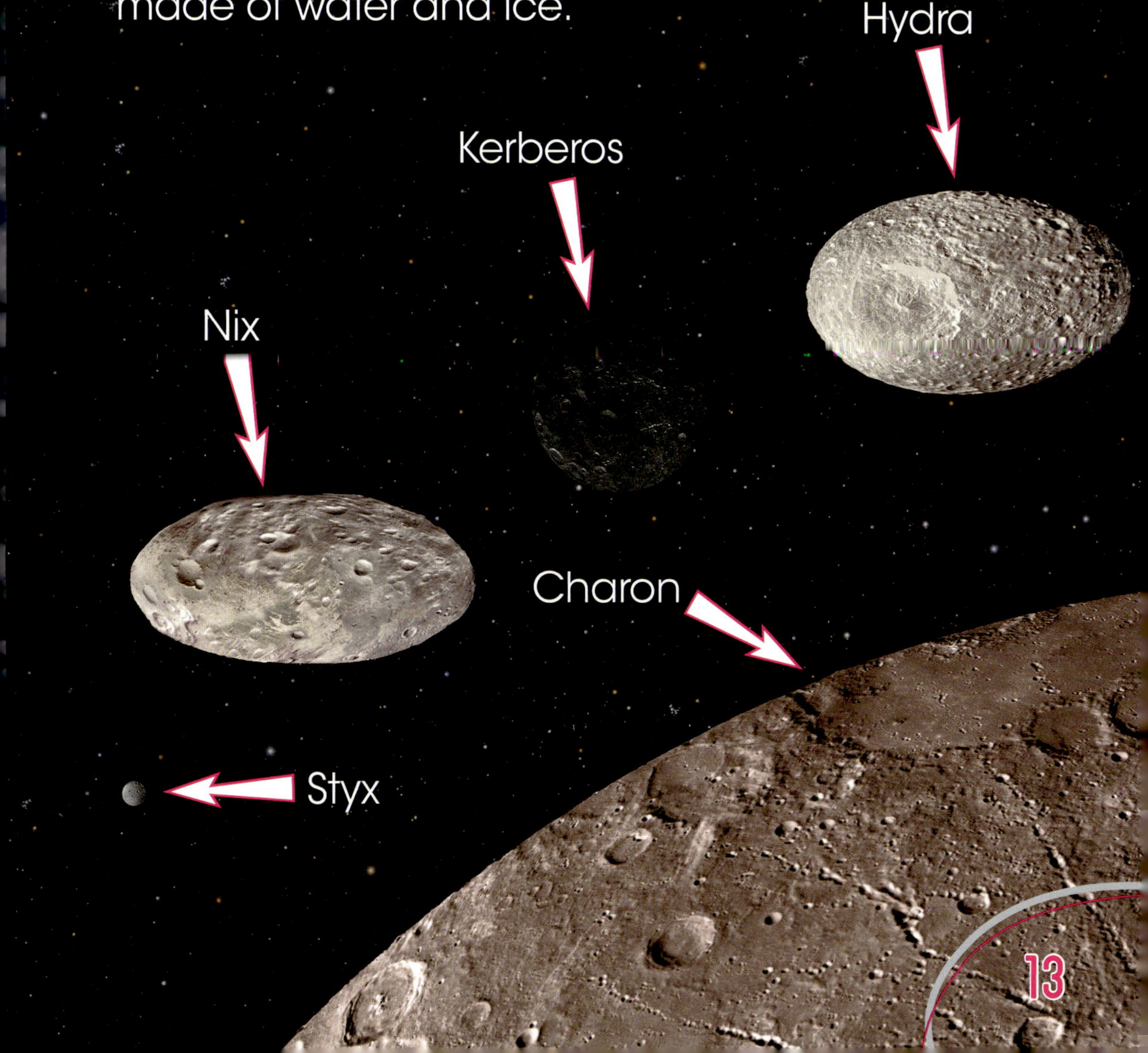

Pluto's closest moon is Charon. It was discovered in 1978, and Nix and Hydra were found in 2005. A very powerful **telescope** was used to discover Kerberos and Styx in 2011 and 2012.

Pluto and Charon are 12,200 miles (19,640 km) away from each other.

STUDYING PLUTO

Pluto and its moons are very hard to see from Earth, even through a powerful telescope. The *New Horizons* probe was launched in 2006 to get a closer look at the dwarf planet. It took nine years to travel from Earth to Pluto!

A probe sends pictures of bodies in space back to Earth. This is just one way probes help people learn about space.

The *New Horizons* probe sent pictures of Pluto to scientists in 2015. Pluto was the first dwarf planet to be explored by a probe.

Because Pluto spins slowly, pictures have only been taken of one side.

Mountains, icy plains, and bowl-shaped holes called craters were found in the new pictures of Pluto. Some of the dwarf planet's mountains are 11,000 feet (3,500 m) tall. Some photos even show ice **volcanoes**!

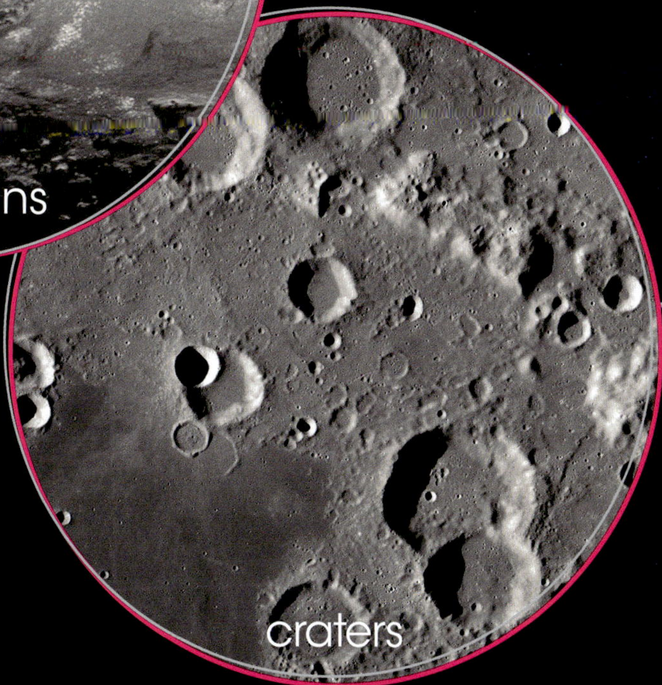

These craters and mountains were discovered in the pictures sent by the *New Horizons* probe.

GLOSSARY

asteroid belt: The area between Mars and Jupiter where most asteroids orbit the sun.

Kuiper Belt: An area of the solar system beyond the orbit of Neptune, believed to contain many comets, asteroids, and other small bodies made of ice.

layer: One part of something lying over or under another.

orbit: To travel in a circle or oval around something.

solar system: The sun and all the space objects that orbit it, including planets and their moons.

telescope: An instrument used to view distant objects, such as the planets in space.

volcano: An opening in the ground through which hot, liquid rock sometimes flows.

FOR MORE INFORMATION

Websites

NASA Space Place: Peculiar Pluto
spaceplace.nasa.gov/ice-dwarf/en/
NASA's website has cool photos of and fun facts about Pluto.

National Geographic Kids: Dwarf Planets
kids.nationalgeographic.com/explore/space/dwarf-planets/#pluto-heart.jpg
This website allows visitors to learn more about Pluto and other dwarf planets.

Books

Buckley, James, Jr. *Curious About Pluto*. New York, NY: Grosset & Dunlap, 2016.

Glaser, Chaya. *Pluto: The Icy Dwarf Planet*. New York, NY: Bearport Publishing, 2015.

Lawrence, Ellen. *Pluto and the Dwarf Planets*. Cornwall, UK: Ruby Tuesday Books, 2014.

INDEX